WHEN I THINK OF YOU

WHEN I THINK
OF YOU

Written and Edited by Jill Wolf

ISBN 0-89954-443-6
Copyright © 1992 Antioch Publishing Company
Yellow Springs, Ohio 45387

Printed in the U.S.A.

CONTENTS

Great thoughts come from the heart.
—Marquis de Vauvenargues

*There is an exchange of thoughts and feeling
which is happily alike in speech and in silence.*
—Henry van Dyke

Joy is not in things; it is in us.
—Richard Wagner

*You know my supreme happiness at having
one on earth whom I can call a friend.*
—Charles Lamb

...while I think on thee, dear friend,
All losses are restored and sorrows end.
—William Shakespeare

No soul is desolate as long as there is a human
being for whom it can feel trust and reverence.
—George Eliot

...to know someone who thinks and feels
with us, and who, though distant, is close
to us in spirit, this makes the earth
for us an inhabited garden.
—Johann Wolfgang von Goethe

I thank my God every time I remember you.
Philippians 1:3 (NIV)

INSPIRATION

I think of you often—in the midst of a busy day and in the quiet moments when I am alone.

Where'er I am, by shore, at sea,
I think of thee.
                    —David M. Moir

I keep thinking about you every few minutes all day.
                    —Walt Whitman

No night is good for me
That does not hold a thought of thee.
                    —Silas W. Mitchell

When I think of you, I think good thoughts
of all the wonderful things you have brought
into my life.

Great thoughts come from the heart.
                    —*Marquis de Vauvenargues*

...whatever is true, whatever is noble, whatever
is right, whatever is pure, whatever is lovely,
whatever is admirable—if anything is excellent
or praiseworthy—think about such things.
                    Philippians 4:8 (NIV)

My friend is that one whom I can associate
with my choicest thought.
                    —*Henry David Thoreau*

When I think of you, I realize how much richer my life is because of you. The very thought of you is a treasured possession that I hold in my mind and my heart.

The glow of one warm thought is to me worth more than money.

—*Thomas Jefferson*

The thoughts that come often unsought, and, as it were, drop into the mind, are commonly the most valuable of any we have.

—*John Locke*

What wealth it is to have such friends that we cannot think of them without elevation.

—*Henry David Thoreau*

When I think of you, I am aware of how my life has changed for the better since I have known you, and how you have given me a new perspective and a positive outlook on everything.

Through thee alone the sky is arched,
Through thee the rose is red;
All things through thee take nobler form,
And look beyond the earth,
The mill-round of our fate appears
A sun-path in thy worth.
Me too thy nobleness has taught
To master my despair;
The fountains of my hidden life
Are through thy friendship fair.
—Ralph Waldo Emerson

When I think of you, I recognize what an inspiration you are to me and how I'm a better person for knowing you.

TOUCHING SHOULDERS

There's a comforting thought at the
    close of the day,
When I'm weary and lonely and sad,
That sort of grips hold of my crusty
    old heart
And bids it be merry and glad.
It gets in my soul and it drives out
    the blues,
And finally thrills through and through.
It is just a sweet memory that chants
    the refrain:
"I'm glad I touch shoulders with you!"

Did you know you were brave, did you
    know you were strong?
Did you know there was one leaning hard?
Did you know that I waited and
    listened and prayed,
And was cheered by your simplest word?
Did you know that I longed for that
    smile on your face,
For the sound of your voice ringing true?
Did you know I grew stronger and
    better because
I had merely touched shoulders with you?

I am glad that I live, that I battle and strive
For the place that I know I must fill;
I am thankful for sorrows; I'll meet
    with a grin
What fortune may send, good or ill.
I may not have wealth, I may not be great,
But I know I shall always be true,
For I have in my life that courage
    you gave
When once I rubbed shoulders with you.

                              —*Author Unknown*

UNDERSTANDING

*When I think of you, I'm intrigued by the
mystery of you and by the wonder of getting to
know you and discovering all the little things
about you that make you uniquely you. Yet I
also feel that we can respect each other's
secrets and privacy and still be close.*

A wonderful fact to reflect upon, that every
human creature is constituted to be that pro-
found secret and mystery to every other.
—Charles Dickens

The human heart has hidden treasures,
In secret kept, in silence sealed;—
The thoughts, the hopes, the dreams,
    the pleasures,
Whose charms were broken if revealed.
—Charlotte Brontë

When I think of you, I think of the comfortable silences between us that show we can communicate without words because we understand one another so well.

One of the most beautiful qualities of true friendship is to understand and to be understood.

—Seneca

Love understands love; it needs no talk.

—Frances Ridley Havergal

The language of friendship is not words, but meanings. It is an intelligence above language.

—Henry David Thoreau

When I think of you, I feel that I want to open up to you and that I must confide in you. I want to tell you my deepest feelings and concerns because I know you will listen and you will care.

The happiest moments my heart knows are those in which it is pouring forth its affections to a few esteemed characters.

—*Thomas Jefferson*

If we are truly prudent we shall cherish those noblest and happiest of our tendencies—to love and to confide.

—*Edward Bulwer-Lytton*

I can never close my lips where I have opened my heart.

—*Charles Dickens*

*When I think of you, I always file away some
special thought I want to share with you—the
latest news, a lovely poem or saying, a little
joke or story—anything I know you'll enjoy
or appreciate as I do.*

My heart shall be thy garden.
    Come, my own,
Into thy garden; thine be happy hours
Among my fairest thoughts,
    my tallest flowers,
From root to crowning petal
    thine alone.
                                        —*Alice Meynell*

If, instead of a gem or even a flower, we would
cast the gift of a lovely thought into the heart
of a friend, that would be giving as the angels
give.
                                        —*George Macdonald*

When I think of you, I want you to know that
very moment how much you mean to me and I
can hardly wait to see you to tell you so.

Do not keep the alabaster boxes of your love
and tenderness sealed up until your friends are
dead. Fill their lives with sweetness. Speak
approving, cheering words while their ears can
hear them, and while their hearts can be
thrilled and made happier by them.

—George W. Childs

I think we had the chief of all love's joys
Only in knowing that we loved each other.

—George Eliot

This is the world of light and speech, and I
shall take leave to tell you that you are very
dear.

—George Eliot

When I think of you, I remember the way you listen to me, the way you share your own thoughts with me, and the way we can talk about anything and everything.

The very best thing is good talk, and the thing that helps it most, is friendship. How it dissolves the barriers that divide us, and loosens all constraints, and diffuses itself like some fine old cordial through all the veins of life—this feeling that we understand and trust each other, and wish each other heartily well! Everything into which it really comes is good. It transforms letter-writing from a task to a pleasure. It makes music a thousand times more sweet. The people who play and sing not *at us,* but *to us,* how delightful it is to listen to them! Yes, there is a talkability that can express itself even without words. There is an exchange of thoughts and feeling which is happily alike in speech and in silence. It is quietness pervaded with friendship.

—*Henry van Dyke*

When I think of you, I'm amazed at how we think of the same things at the same time—as if we shared one heart, one mind, one soul.

There's something so beautiful in coming on one's very own inmost thoughts in another. In one way it's one of the greatest pleasures one has.

—Olive Schreiner

Love is but the discovery of ourselves in others, and the delight in the recognition.

—Alexander Smith

Two souls with but a single thought, Two hearts that beat as one.

—Von Münch Bellinghausen

When I think of you, I'm glad that we have so much in common and that we both like so many of the same things, for it gives us so much to share and makes everything more special.

It is hard to believe that anything is worthwhile, unless...what is infinitely precious to us is precious alike to another mind.
                                        —*George Eliot*

The thought that would delight thy
Love must first have delighted thyself.
                              —*Richard Garnett*

Whatever one possesses, becomes of double value, when we have the opportunity of sharing it with others.
                                        —*Bouilly*

HAPPINESS

When I think of you, I think of the happiness
we share and the good times we have together.
I love your laugh, your smile, and the way
you enjoy life—not just the big moments,
but the quiet joys and the little things, too.

Joy is not in things; it is in us.
                              —Richard Wagner

The happiness of life is made up of minute
fractions...a kiss or smile, a kind look, a
heartfelt compliment...

                         —Samuel Taylor Coleridge

What sunshine is to flowers, smiles are to
humanity.

                              —Joseph Addison

When I think of you, I think of sunshine and
blue skies, for you brighten each day and
lighten up my outlook on life.

My friend peers in on me with merry
Wise face, and though the sky stay dim,
The very light of day, the very
Sun's self comes in with him.
                    —*Charles A. Swinburne*

Everyone must have felt that a cheerful friend
is like a sunny day, which sheds its brightness
on all around...

                    —*Lord Avebury*

What joy is better than the news of friends?
                    —*Robert Browning*

When I think of you, I appreciate how much sweeter life is and how much more beautiful the world has become for me because of you.

Love planted a rose,
And the world turned sweet,
Where the wheatfield blows,
Love planted a rose.
Up the mill-wheel's prose
Ran a music beat.
Love planted a rose,
And the world turned sweet.
—*Katharine Lee Bates*

When I think of you, I realize that my life was
full, but now it has overflowed with reasons
for joy and happiness.

My life is a bowl which is mine to brim
With loveliness old and new.
So I fill its clay from stem to rim
With you, dear heart, with you.

My life is a pool which can only hold
One star and a glimpse of blue.
But the blue and the little lamp of gold
Are you, dear heart, are you.

My life is a homing bird that flies
Through the starry dusk and dew
Home to the heaven of your true eyes,
Home, dear heart, to you.

—*May Riley Smith*

When I think of you, I picture your face, your eyes, your smile—and I realize how beautiful you are to me.

A good face is a letter of recommendation, as a good heart is a letter of credit.
—*Edward Bulwer-Lytton*

Whatsoe'er thy birth,
Thou wert a beautiful thought,
    and softly bodied forth.
—*Lord Byron*

When I think of you, I cherish the memories
of moments we're shared, from the little
everyday things to the very special occasions.

Still are the thoughts to memory dear.
                              —*Sir Walter Scott*

The hours I spent with thee, dear heart,
Are as a string of pearls to me;
I count them over, every one apart,
My rosary, my rosary.
                        —*Robert Cameron Rogers*

God has given us memory that we might have
roses in December.

                              —*J. M. Barrie*

When I think of you, I know that the thoughts
of our happiness, past and present, are so dear
because they promise more such moments for
the future.

We must always have old memories and
young hopes.

—Arsène Houssaye

A memory without blot or contamination
must be an exquisite treasure, an inexhaustible
source of pure refreshment.

—Charlotte Brontë

I count myself in nothing else so happy,
As in a soul rememb'ring my good friends...

—William Shakespeare

When I think of you, I feel that no matter what
happens, I will always have happy memories
of you. Nothing can make them fade; nothing
can take them away.

Let Fate do her worst; there are relics
  of joy,
Bright dreams of the past, which she
  cannot destroy;
Which come in the night-time of sorrow
  and care,
And bring back the features that joy
  used to wear.
Long, long be my heart with such
  memories filled,
Like the vase in which roses have once
  been distilled—
You may break, you may shatter the
  vase if you will,
But the scent of the roses will hang
  round it still.

                              —*Thomas Moore*

When I think of you, it is my heart that remembers, and it remembers best.

If stores of dry and learned lore we gain,
We keep them in the memory of the brain;
Names, things, and facts—whate'er we
    knowledge call—
There is the common ledger for them all;
And images on this cold surface traced
Make slight impression, and are soon
    effaced.
But we've a page, more glowing and
    more bright,
On which our friendship and our love
    to write;
That these may never from the soul depart,
We trust them to the memory of the heart.
There is no dimming, no effacement there;
Each new pulsation keeps the record clear;
Warm, golden letters all the tablet fill,
Nor lose their lustre till the heart
    stands still.

—Daniel Webster

When I think of you, that thought reminds me
that you make up for any mere material thing
I may lack, for I have something infinitely
more valuable in knowing you.

When in disgrace with Fortune and men's
    eyes,
I all alone beweep my outcast state,
And trouble deaf heaven with my bootless
    cries,
And look upon myself and curse my fate,
Wishing me like to one more rich in hope,
Featur'd like him, like him with friends
    possess'd,
Desiring this man's art, and that man's scope,
With what I most enjoy contented least;
Yet in these thoughts myself almost despising,
Haply I think on thee, and then my state,
Like to the lark at break of day arising
From sullen earth, sings hymns at
    heaven's gate;
For thy sweet love rememb'red such
    wealth brings
That then I scorn to change my state
    with kings.

                       —William Shakespeare

LOVE AND FRIENDSHIP

When I think of you, I think of a cozy place
beside the fire on a rainy day or about my
favorite old coat or jeans, because we are
so comfortable together, like old friends.
I appreciate the way I can be myself with you.

My coat and I live comfortably together. It has
assumed all my wrinkles, does not hurt me
anywhere, has moulded itself on my deformi-
ties and is complacent to all my movements,
and I only feel its presence because it keeps me
warm. Old coats and old friends are the same
thing.

—Victor Hugo

Perhaps the most delightful friendships are
those in which there is much agreement, much
disputation, and yet more personal liking.

—George Eliot

When I think of you, I think of you as my best
friend and I recognize how much that friend-
ship means to me.

If words came as readily as ideas and ideas
as feeling, I could say ten hundred kindly
things. You know my supreme happiness
at having one on earth whom I can call
a friend.

—Charles Lamb

When the heart overflows with gratitude,
or with any other sweet and sacred sentiment,
what is the word to which it would give
utterance? A friend.

—Walter Savage Landor

When I think of you, I hope that you are
thinking of me as your best friend, too.

Think of me as your friend, I pray,
And call me by a loving name;
I will not care what others say,
If only you remain the same.
I will not care how dark the night,
I will not care how wild the storm,
Your love will fill my heart with light
And shield me close and keep me warm.

Think of me as your friend, I pray,
For else my life is little worth:
So shall your memory light my way,
Although we meet no more on earth.
For while I know your faith secure,
I ask no happier fate to see:
Thus to be loved by one so pure
Is honor rich enough for me.

—*William Winter*

When I think of you, I feel the warmth that love and friendship bring—and I feel I'm doubly blessed.

A friendship that like love is warm;
A love like friendship steady.
                              —*Thomas Moore*

Like everything breathing of kindness—
Like these is the love of a friend.
                              —*A. P. Stanley*

What brings joy to the heart is not so much
the friend's gift as the friend's love.
                              —*St. Aelred of Rievaulx*

*When I think of you, I feel as if I have a place
to go when everyone else has turned me
away—a place of security and rest. I think that
whenever I am with you, I am home.*

Where we love is home,
Home that our feet may leave,
   but not our hearts.
        —Oliver Wendell Holmes

Every house where love abides
And friendship is a guest,
Is surely home, and home-sweet-home:
For there the heart can rest.
           —Henry van Dyke

Sweet is the smile of home; the mutual look,
Where hearts are of each other sure.

—John Keble

Something like home that is not home is to be
desired; it is found in the house of a friend.

—Sir William Temple

Home is where there's one to love!
Home is where there's one to love us!

—Charles Swain

Traveling in the company of those we love
is home in motion.

—Leigh Hunt

COMFORT AND KINDNESS

When I think of you, I think of how you saw
something in me that others overlooked, and
of how you took the time to get to know me
and to give me a chance.

Like everyone else I feel the need of relations
and friendship, of affection, of friendly inter-
course, and I am not made of stone or iron, so I
cannot miss these things without feeling...a
void and deep need. I tell you this to let you
know how much good your visit has done me.

—*Vincent van Gogh*

Our inward thoughts, do they ever show
outwardly? There may be a great fire in our
soul, and...passers-by see only a little bit of
smoke coming through the chimney, and pass
on their way.

—*Vincent van Gogh*

*When I think of you, my troubles seem smaller,
my problems seem solvable, and my losses are
things I can recover from.*

When to the sessions of sweet silent thought
I summon up remembrance of things past,
I sigh the lack of many a thing I sought,
And with old woes new wail
        my dear time's waste:
Then can I drown an eye, unused to flow,
For precious friends hid in
    death's dateless night,
And weep afresh love's long since
        cancell'd woe,
And moan the expense of many
        a vanish'd sight:
Then can I grieve at grievances foregone,
And heavily from woe to woe tell o'er
The sad account of fore-bemoaned moan,
Which I new pay as if not paid before.
But if the while I think on thee, dear friend,
All losses are restored and sorrows end.

—*William Shakespeare*

When I think of you, I think of all the nice things you have done for me and how you have not only shown me kindness, but how to be kind.

Blessed is the influence of one true, loving human soul on another.

—*George Eliot*

A good heart is better than all the heads in the world.

—*Edward Bulwer-Lytton*

Guard within yourself that treasure, kindness.

—*George Sand*

When I think of you, I recognize how fair and honest you are, yet just how kind and forgiving you always are, too.

Oh, the comfort, the inexpressible comfort of feeling safe with a person, having neither to weigh thoughts nor measure words, but pouring them all right out, just as they are, chaff and grain together; certain that a faithful hand will take and sift them, keep what is worth keeping, and then with the breath of kindness blow the rest away.

—Dinah Maria Craik

When I think of you, I think of how willing
you are to help and how you seem to know
just the right thing to do when life gets
difficult. And, most of all, you know when
to help and when to let me stand on my own.

What do we live for, if it is not to make life
less difficult to each other?

—*George Eliot*

No one is useless in this world who lightens
the burden of it to anyone else.

—*Charles Dickens*

Often we can help each other the most by
leaving each other alone; at other times we
need the hand-grasp and the word of cheer.

—*Elbert Hubbard*

TRUST AND RESPECT

When I think of you, I feel that I can trust
you. I respect and admire you and I appreciate
your honesty. I know you would never do an
unworthy thing or hurt anyone.

We meet on the broad pathway of good faith
and good will; no advantage shall be taken on
either side, but all shall be openness and love.

—William Penn

No soul is desolate as long as there is a human
being for whom it can feel trust and reverence.

—George Eliot

When I think of you, I am grateful for the loyalty you show through good times and bad times. I know you will always be there for me.

We have been friends together,
In sunshine and in shade...
—*Caroline Norton*

There are evergreen men and women in the world, praise be to God!—not many of them, but a few. The sun of our prosperity makes the green of their friendship no brighter, the frost of our adversity kills not the leaves of their affection.

—*Jerome K. Jerome*

I know not whether our names will be immortal; I am sure our friendship will.
—*Walter Savage Landor*

When I think of you, I feel that no matter what happens, we will always be in each other's thoughts, minds, and hearts.

Our great thoughts, our great affections, the truths of our life, never leave us.
                    —*William Makepeace Thackeray*

And Love can never lose its own!
                    —*John Greenleaf Whittier*

Thought alone is eternal.
                    —*Owen Meredith*

And, when the stream
Which overflowed the soul was passed away,
A consciousness remained that it had left,
Deposited upon the silent shore
Of memory, images and precious thoughts,
That shall not die, and cannot be destroyed.

—*William Wordsworth*

When I think of you, I am affected by your
inner strength, dignity, and perseverance.
Your courage makes me feel that we can
stand up to life's difficulties and endure.

When our two souls stand up
   erect and strong,
Face to face, silent, drawing
   nigh and nigher,
Until the lengthening wings
   break into fire
At either curvèd point,—
   what bitter wrong
Can the earth do to us,
   that we should not long
Be here contented?
   —*Elizabeth Barrett Browning*

LONELINESS AND LONGING

When I think of you, I am already planning
for and looking forward to the next time we
will see each other. I miss you every moment
we are not together.

My hand is lonely for your clasping, dear;
My ear is tired waiting for your call.
I want your strength to help, your laugh
   to cheer;
Heart, soul and senses need you, one and all.
I droop without your full, frank sympathy;
We ought to be together—you and I;
We want each other so, to comprehend
The dream, the hope, things planned,
   or seen, or wrought.
Companion, comforter and guide and friend,
As much as love asks love, does
   thought ask thought.
Life is so short, so fast the lone hours fly,
We ought to be together, you and I.

            —Henry Alford

When I think of you, it makes the world seem
less empty, cold, and lonely, just to know
you are in it.

The world is so empty if one thinks only of
mountains, rivers, and cities; but to know
someone who thinks and feels with us, and
who, though distant, is close to us in spirit,
this makes the earth for us an inhabited
garden.

—*Johann Wolfgang von Goethe*

When I think of you, even though you are
not with me, just the thought of you makes
me feel that I have someone on my side,
out there pulling for me, giving me support.

To love and to be loved, is the greatest
happiness. If I lived under the burning sun
of the equator, it would be pleasure for me
to think that there were many human beings on
the other side of the world who regarded and
respected me; I could not live if I were alone
upon the earth, and cut off from the remembrance of my fellow-creatures. It is not that a
man has occasion often to fall back upon the
kindness of his friends; perhaps he may never
experience the necessity of doing so; but we
are governed by our imaginations, and they
stand there as a solid and impregnable bulwark
against all the evils of life.

—Sydney Smith

When I think of you and you're not with me,
sometimes I feel lost or as if a part of myself
is missing. Although I know you are with me
in spirit, I search for a tangible sign of you to
reassure myself. And I find myself wishing we
had more time to be together.

Never the time and the place
And the loved one all together!
>   —*Robert Browning*

High thoughts and noble in all lands
Help me; my soul is fed by such.
But ah, the touch of lips and hands—
The human touch!
Warm, vital, close, life's symbols dear,—
These need I most, and now, and here.
>   —*Richard Burton*

When I think of you and we are far apart, we are, in a way, closer together, for then I think of you even more.

Friendship, like love...may be increased by short intermissions. What we have missed... we value more when it is regained.

—*Samuel Johnson*

Because of a friend, life is a little stronger, fuller, more gracious thing for the friend's existence, whether he be near or far. If the friend is close at hand, that is best; but if he is far away he still is there to think of, to wonder about, to hear from, to write to, to share life and experience with, to serve, to honor, to admire, to love.

—*Arthur C. Benson*

When I think of you, I am not alone—
my thoughts of you keep me company.

They are never alone that are accompanied
with noble thoughts.

                              —Sir Philip Sidney

THANKFULNESS

When I think of you, I am so glad that you came into my life. I am thankful for the gift of you.

I thank my God every time I remember you.
Philippians 1:3 (NIV)

I awoke this morning with devout thanksgiving for my friends, the old and the new.
—*Ralph Waldo Emerson*

Friendship consists of forgetting what one gives and remembering what one receives.
—*Alexander Dumas*

*When I think of you, I wish with all my heart
that I could protect you and shelter you from
anything bad and make everything good
happen for you.*

Certain thoughts are prayers. There are
moments when, whatever be the attitude of the
body, the soul is on its knees.

—*Victor Hugo*

It is love that asks, that seeks, that knocks, that
finds, and that is faithful to what it finds.

—*St. Augustine*

Dear friend, I pray that you may enjoy good
health and that all may go well with you...

3 John:2 (NIV)

When I think of you, I say a little prayer for you and ask God to bless you.

...if ever fondest prayer
For other's weal avail'd on high,
Mine will not all be lost in air,
But waft thy name beyond the sky.
                              —*Lord Byron*

God, whom I serve with my whole heart...is
my witness how constantly I remember you
in my prayers...

Romans 1:9,10 (NIV)

"The Lord bless you and keep you;
    the Lord make His face shine upon you
    and be gracious to you;
    the Lord turn His face toward you
    and give you peace."

Numbers 6:24-26 (NIV)

I SAID A PRAYER FOR YOU TODAY

I said a prayer for you today
And know God must have heard;
I felt the answer in my heart
Although He spoke not a word.

I didn't ask for wealth or fame
(I knew you wouldn't mind);
I asked for priceless treasures rare
Of a more lasting kind.

I prayed that He'd be near to you
At the start of each new day,
To grant you health and blessings fair,
And friends to share your way.

I asked for happiness for you
In all things great and small,
But that you'd know His loving care
I prayed the most of all.

—Author Unknown

When I think of you, I want to give you in return what you have given me, and I want you to be as happy as you have made me.

To love is to find pleasure in the happiness of the person loved.

—*Baron von Leibnitz*